365+ Greatest Inspirational Quotes on Mindset, Motivation, Happiness and Success

Sneha Rawat

This book is dedicated to every soul who does not pray for an easy life, but for a stronger character

Introduction

It all began when I was at the lowest point in my life. I was dead broke financially with 27$ in my bank account. I was working multiple jobs to support my family. My relationship with friends and family were getting worse. I was constantly bitching about the negative things that were around me and the mess I was in. Whenever there was something wrong with my life, I would either make excuses or blame others for what I faced. I was basically saying that anything bad happening in my life is because of "X" and there's nothing I can do about it.

It all changed one day, when I was walking down the streets, an old and dusty flyer grabbed my attention which quoted,

"If you could kick the person in the pants responsible for most of your trouble, you wouldn't sit for a month."
~Theodore Roosevelt

Those sentences struck me hard. For the next few days, I thought about it many times. I spoke those words to myself as I really meant them. I understood that I am responsible for everything happening to or around me, whether I like it or not.

Once my mind became synchronized with this idea since then those words guided my decisions every single day. Two years then, I ran two different firms which did a total business of $1.5Million last year. My relations are much better now. I am happy, fulfilled and healthy today just because I learned many powerful ideas during my journey which changed my mindset that then changed my whole life.

People around me now ask what turned a dead broke lady into a millionaire in just two years, and I tell them there are three most valuable lessons that life taught me:

First: "Words have power. Words are power."
"You can change your world by changing

your words... Remember, death and life are in the power of the tongue."
~Joel Osteen

Second: "Abracadabra: I will create as I speak"
"Words, when said and articulated in right way, can change someone's mind. They can alter someone's belief. World have power to bring someone from the slumps of life and make a successful person out of them or destroy someone's happiness using only your words."
~Mohammed Qahtani

Third: "Words are most powerful to create change when your subconscious mind accepts it as real"

The human mind is considered to have two parts, conscious mind, and subconscious mind. The conscious mind is logical part and all the mental activities that require effortful mental activities are made by the conscious part of our mind. Subconscious mind is also called subjective mind and all the activities that are automatic and require little or no effort are performed by subconscious part of our mind. Scientist estimated that about 95% of what we do is controlled by our subconscious mind.

You must synchronize your conscious part of mind with the subconscious part to produce great results.
Let's take an example to understand it better. When you had your first driving lesson you would have found it very difficult to manage all the necessary operations, it is because your mind was experiencing an unfamiliar situation and most of the work was done by the conscious mind. But once you get used to driving you can perform many operations without even noticing them and this is because your brain had experienced those operations many times before and now your subconscious mind does it automatically.

So if you want your subconscious mind to work in your favor you must instill empowering ideas into it. The subconscious mind accepts an idea for real when you repeatedly impose that idea on your conscious mind. This process is slow and meandering but once you learn this and embed your mind with great ideas your life will never be the same ever.

I must admit when I started my journey it was not that easy. When I opened my first company everyone around me told that the market is very saturated, my ideas were shoddy and many things that I could not even remember. Look I am here to remind you that history has not just been read but also been written by the people with passion, imagination, and dreams.

Why this book?

When I learned all the three lessons, I started my journey in search of the most powerful set of words ever spoken which could change anyone's mind. What I have found is so valuable that if you use it in the right manner you will not be the same person a year from now.

The quotations in the book will motivate you to do best but here the major goal here is not only motivation but also to inspiration you to be a better version of yourself. The information in this book is designed in such a way that every quotation will enlighten you with immense wisdom. Some lessons are so important that must be repeated persistently. So What I have done, is used different quotations to present the same principle.

How to use this book?

If you go through the whole book once it would barely do you any good to you. In that way, you may get the information but not the wisdom that can only be achieved after the implementation of the stated information. As Albert Einstein once said "Any fool can know. The point is to understand."

Understand, this book is not a onetime
event it should be your one year journey
at least. Give 5 minutes daily to this book
so you can learn something new each
day.

You can either read one quote each
day, write it down and speak those words
to yourself again and again so that your
subconscious mind accepts it and it
becomes your automatic behavior, or if
you want to go fast read two or three
quotes each day but make sure you
repeat those thoughts enough so that
they become part of your mindset.

Start each day with powerful words of
wisdom and let it guide you to take
action, overcome fear, boost your self-
esteem and create success.

Let's start your journey to be the best version of yourself with a short and inspiring story which helped me to stay focused on my goals no matter what I went through.

This was a man who failed in business at age of 21; was defeated in a legislative race at age 22; failed again in business at age 24; overcame the death of his sweetheart at age 26; had a nervous breakdown at age 27; lost a congressional race at age 34; lost a senatorial race at age 45; failed in an effort to become vice-president at age 47; lost a senatorial race at age 49; and was elected president of the United States at age 52.
This man was Abraham Lincoln.

1

"I failed a key primary school test two times;
I failed three times for the middle schools for
three years;
I tried and failed in the universities so I
applied for jobs thirty times got rejected;
I went to even KFC when they came to China
24 people went for the job 23 people accepted, I
was the only one who got rejected;
I applied for Harvard for ten times rejected;
I think we have to get used to rejection. The
only thing. Never give up."
~Jack Ma is the Chairman of Alibaba Group
and the richest man in China

2

"I've missed more than 9000 shots in my
career.
I've lost almost 300 games.
26 times, I've been trusted to take the game-
winning shot and missed.
I've failed over and over and over again in
my life. And that is why I succeed."
~Michael Jordan is considered as greatest
basketball player of all time

3
"We must all either wear out or rust out,
every one of us.
My choice is to wear out."
~Theodore Roosevelt Jr. served as the 26th
President of the United States

4
"If it wasn't hard, everyone would do it.
It's the hard that makes it great."
~Tom Hanks, American actor and filmmaker

5
"No one is you and that is your biggest
power."
~Dave Grohl, American musician and
founder of the rock band
"Foo Fighters"

6
"Strength is life,
Weakness is death."
~Swami Vivekananda was an Indian Hindu
monk and considered as a key figure in the
introduction of the Indian philosophies of
Vedanta and Yoga to the Western world

7
"Some people dream of success,
While others wake up and work hard at it."
~Winston Churchill served as Prime Minister
of the United Kingdom from 1940 to 1945 and
again from 1951 to 1955

8
"If people knew how hard I worked to get my
mastery, it wouldn't seem so wonderful at all."
~Michelangelo was an Italian painter,
architect, and poet and has been considered as
one of the greatest artists of all time

9
"The journey of a thousand miles begins with
one step."
~Lao Tzu was an ancient Chinese
philosopher and writer

10
"I've come to believe that all my past failure
and frustrations were actually laying the
foundation for the understandings that have
created the new level of living I now enjoy."
~Tony Robbins is an American author,
entrepreneur,
Philanthropist and life coach

11
"Passion is the thing that will help you create
the highest expression of your talent."
~Larry Smith is an American author, editor,
and best known for developing the best-selling
book series
"Six-Word Memoirs"

12
"As far as I can tell, it's just about letting the
universe know what you want and then working
toward it while letting go of how it comes to
pass."
~Jim Carrey is a Canadian-American actor,
comedian, and best known for the movie
"The Truman Show"

13
"What you have to learn is to fold early when
the odds are against you or if you have a big
edge, back it heavily because you don't get a big
edge often. Opportunity comes, but it doesn't
come often, so seize it when it does come."
~Charlie Munger is vice chairman of
Berkshire Hathaway with a net worth of
US$1.56 billion on August 2017

14

"I am very happy because I have conquered
myself and not the world.
I am very happy because I have loved the
world and not myself."
~Sri Chinmoy was a spiritual teacher who
dedicated his life in service to aspiring humanity

15

"Always go with your passions.
Never ask yourself if it's realistic or not."
~Deepak Chopra is an American author,
public speaker and wealthiest figures in
alternative medicine

16

"Render more service than that which you are
paid and you will soon be paid for more than
you render.
The law of increasing returns takes care of
this."
~Napoleon Hill was an American self-help
author and famous for
"Think and Grow Rich"

17
"To move the world, we must first move
ourselves."
~Socrates was a classical Greek philosopher
credited as one of the founders of Western
philosophy

18
"A man has to learn that he cannot command
things, but that he can command himself; that
he cannot coerce the wills of others, but that he
can mold and master his own will: and things
serve him who serves Truth; people seek
guidance of him who is master of himself."
~James Allen was a British philosophical
writer and best known for the book
"As a Man Thinketh"

19
"The future was uncertain, absolutely, and
there were many hurdles, twists, and turns to
come, but as long as I kept moving forward, one
foot in front of the other, the voices of fear and
shame, the messages from those who wanted
me to believe that I wasn't good enough, would
be stilled."
~Chris Gardner is an American
Entrepreneur, motivational speaker and author
of
"The Pursuit of Happyness"

20

"The pain you feel today will be the strength
you feel tomorrow."
~Arnold Schwarzenegger is actor, politician,
and former professional bodybuilder and served
two terms as the 38th Governor of California

21

"Fearlessness is like a muscle.
I know from my own life that the more I
exercise it the more natural it becomes to not let
my fears run me."
~Arianna Huffington is a Greek American
author and the co-founder of
"The Huffington Post"

22

"The more you praise and celebrate your life,
the more there is in life to celebrate."
~Oprah Winfrey is an American media
proprietor, talk show host, actress and producer

23
"I really think a champion is defined not by their wins but by how they can recover when they fall."
~Serena Williams is an American professional tennis player and has ranked world's No. 1 in singles on eight separate occasions over the last 15 years by Women's Tennis Association (WTA)

24
"Being realistic is the most common path to mediocrity."
~Will Smith is an American actor and according to Newsweek April 2007 he is "the most powerful actor in Hollywood"

25
"It is a universal principle that you get more of what you think about, talk about, and feel strongly about."
~Jack Canfield is an American author and best known for the book series "Chicken Soup for the Soul"

26
"We all live with the objective of being happy;
our lives are all different and yet the same."
~Anne Frank was a German-born diarist, one
of the most discussed Jewish victims of the
Holocaust and Time Magazine named her
among The Most Important People of the 20th
Century

27
"We think, mistakenly, that success is the
result of the amount of time we put in at work,
instead of the quality of time we put in."
~Arianna Huffington is a Greek American
author and the co-founder of
"The Huffington Post"

28
"There are no mistakes in life, only lessons.
There is no such thing as a negative
experience, only opportunities to grow, learn
and advance along the road of self-mastery.
From struggle comes strength.
Even pain can be a wonderful teacher."
~Robin Sharma is a Canadian writer and best
known for the book
"The Monk Who Sold His Ferrari"

29
"Look at your 5 closest friends.
Those 5 friends are who you are.
If you don't like who you are then you know
what you have to do."
~Will Smith is an American actor and
according to Newsweek April 2007 he is "the
most powerful actor in Hollywood"

30
"Everybody in the world is seeking happiness
and there is one sure way to find it.
That is by controlling your thoughts.
Happiness doesn't depend on outward
conditions.
It depends on inner conditions."
~Dale Carnegie was an American writer and
very famous for the bestselling book "how to
win friends and influence people"

31
"If you don't educate yourself, you'll never get
out of the starting block because you'll spend all
your money making foolish decisions."
~Daymond John is an American
businessman, investor, and founder FUBU

32
"The greatest benefit isn't getting what you
want.
The greatest benefit is what you'll need to
become in order to get what you want."
~Eric Worre is a writer, producer and best
known for the Documentary
"Rise of the Entrepreneur: The Search for a
Better Way"

33
"I believe you have to be willing to be
misunderstood if you're going to innovate."
~Jeff Bezos is an American technology and
retail entrepreneur and best known as the
founder of Amazon.com

34
"The foolish man seeks happiness in the
distance.
The wise grows it under his feet."
~James Oppenheim was an American poet,
novelist and the founder of "The Seven Arts", an
important early 20th-century literary magazine

35
"Only he who has the courage to write the
word 'end' can find the strength to write the
word 'beginning'."
~Zen Proverb

36
"Screw it.
Let's do it."
~Sir Richard Branson is the founder of Virgin
Group, which controls more than 400
companies

37
"Everything negative pressure, challenges; is
all an opportunity for me to rise."
~Kobe Bryant is an American retired
professional basketball player and widely
regarded as one of the greatest basketball
players of all time

38

"The reason people find it so hard to be happy is that they always see the past better than it was, the present worse than it is, and the future less resolved than it will be."
~Marcel Pagnol was a French novelist and regarded as one of France's greatest 20th-century writers

39

"Well done is better than well said."
~Benjamin Franklin was a renowned polymath and one of the Founding Fathers of the United States

40

"The way you think, the way you behave, the way you eat, can influence your life by 30 to 50 years."
~Deepak Chopra is an American author, public speaker and wealthiest figures in alternative medicine

41
"Knowledge can be communicated, but not wisdom.
One can find it, live it, be fortified by it, do wonders through it, but one cannot communicate and teach it."
~Hermann Hesse was a German-born novelist and best-known the book "Siddhartha"

42
"Having a low opinion of yourself is not 'modesty.'
It's self-destruction.
Holding your uniqueness in high regard is not 'egotism.'
It's a necessary precondition to happiness and success."
~Bobbe Sommer is a leading psychotherapist and very famous for writing the book "Psycho-Cybernetics 2000"

43
"When you get into a tight Place and
everything goes against you, until it seems as
though you could not hang on a minute longer,
it is then when you should never give up, for
that is just the place and time when the tide will
turn."
~Harriet Beecher Stowe was an American
author and best known for her novel
"Uncle Tom's Cabin"

44
"Where there's hope, there's life.
It fills us with fresh courage and makes us
strong again."
~Anne Frank was a German-born diarist, one
of the most discussed Jewish victims of the
Holocaust and Time Magazine named her
among The Most Important People of the 20th
Century

45
"What you get by achieving your goals is not
as important as what you become by achieving
your goals."
~Zig Ziglar was an American author and
motivational speaker

46
"There is a saying in Tibetan, "Tragedy
should be utilized as a source of strength."
No matter what sort of difficulties, how
painful experience is, if we lose our hope, that's
our real disaster."
~Tenzin Gyatso is the XIV Dalai Lama

47
"Action without vision is only passing time,
vision without action is merely day dreaming,
but vision with action can change the world."
~Nelson Mandela was a South African anti-
apartheid revolutionary and served as President
of South Africa from 1994 to 1999

48
"Whenever you find yourself on the side of
the majority, it is time to pause and reflect."
~Samuel Langhorne Clemens better known
by his pen name Mark Twain, was an American
writer and humorist

49
"Our imagination is the only limit to what we
can hope to have in the future."
~Charles Kettering was an American inventor
and the holder of 186 patents

50
"Do not spoil what you have by desiring what
you have not; remember that what you now
have was once among the things you only hoped
for."
~Epicurus was an ancient Greek philosopher
who founded a school of philosophy now called
"Epicureanism"

51
"There is only one thing that makes a dream
impossible to achieve: the fear of failure."
~Paulo Coelho is the author of
"The Alchemist"

52
"Failure will never overtake me if my
determination to succeed is strong enough."
~Og Mandino was an American author of
"The Greatest Salesman in the World"

53
"Be willing to go all out, in pursuit of your
dream.
Ultimately it will pay off.
You are more powerful than you think you
are."
~Les Brown is an American motivational
speaker and author

54
"Nothing is impossible, the word itself says
'I'm possible"
~Audrey Hepburn was a film and fashion
icon

55
"If you're never scared or embarrassed or
hurt, it means you never take any chances."
~Rosalyn Drexler is novelist, Obie Award-
winning playwright, and Emmy Award-winning
screenwriter

56
"When we are no longer able to change a
situation, we are challenged to change
ourselves."
~Viktor E Frankl was the author of Man's
search for meaning

57
"Successful people do what unsuccessful
people are not willing to do.
Don't wish it were easier, wish you were
better."
~Jim Rohn was an American entrepreneur,
author, and motivational speaker

58
"What holds most people back isn't the
quality of their ideas, but their lack of faith in
themselves.
You have to live your life as if you are already
where you want to be."
~Russell Simmons is the chairman and CEO
of Rush Communications

59
"I find that the harder I work, the more luck I
seem to have."
~Thomas Jefferson was one of the Founding
Fathers of the United States and served as the
third President of the United States

60
"We cannot choose our external
circumstances, but we can always choose how
we respond to them."
~Epictetus was a Greek Stoic philosopher

61
"A man is literally what he thinks, his
character being the complete sum of all his
thoughts."
~James Allen was a British philosophical
writer and best known for the book
"As a Man Thinketh"

62
"Life begins at the end of your comfort zone."
~Neale Donald Walsch is an American author
of the series
"Conversations with God"

63

"With everything that has happened to you,
you can either feel sorry for yourself or treat
what has happened as a gift.
Everything is either an opportunity to grow
or an obstacle to keep you from growing.
You get to choose."
~Wayne Dyer was an American philosopher,
self-help author, and a motivational speaker

64

"The will to win, the desire to succeed, the
urge to reach your full potential... these are the
keys that will unlock the door to personal
excellence."
~Confucius was a Chinese teacher, politician,
and philosopher

65

"The reason most people never reach their
goals is that they don't define them, or ever
seriously consider them as believable or
achievable.
Winners can tell you where they are going,
what they plan to do along the way, and who
will be sharing the adventure with them."
~Denis Waitley is the best-selling author of
the audio series,
"The Psychology of Winning"

66
"To be successful you must accept all
challenges that come your way.
You can't just accept the ones you like."
~Mike Gafka is Senior WW Business Strategy
Manager at HP Inc.

67
"Chains of habit are too light to be felt until
they are too heavy to be broken."
~Warren Buffett is an American business
magnate and the fourth wealthiest person in the
world

68
"Ask and it will be given to you; seek and you
will find; knock and the door will be opened to
you."
~Jesus Christ, Matthew 7:7

69
"A man can be as great as he wants to be.
If you believe in yourself and have the
courage, the determination, the dedication, the
competitive drive and if you are willing to
sacrifice the little things in life and pay the price
for the things that are worthwhile, it can be
done."
~Vince Lombardi was an American football
player, coach, and executive in the National
Football League

70
"The average person puts only 25% of his
energy and ability into his work. The world
takes off its hat to those who put in more than
50% of their capacity, and stands on its head for
those few and far between souls who devote
100%."
~Andrew Carnegie was a Scottish-American
industrialist and often identified as one of the
richest people ever

71
"If you don't value your time, neither will others. Stop giving away your time and talents. Value what you know and start charging for it."
~Kim Garst is the Founder and CEO of "Boom! Social"

72
"Live as if you were to die tomorrow. Learn as if you were to live forever."
~Mahatma Gandhi was the leader of the Indian independence movement against British rule

73
"Take up one idea. Make that one idea your life – think of it, dream of it, live on that idea. Let the brain, muscles, nerves, every part of your body, be full of that idea, and just leave every other idea alone. This is the way to success."
~ Swami Vivekananda was an Indian Hindu monk and considered as a key figure in the introduction of the Indian philosophies of Vedanta and Yoga to the Western world

74
"You can't connect the dots looking forward;
you can only connect them looking backwards.
So you have to trust that the dots will
somehow connect in your future.
You have to trust in something – your gut,
destiny, life, karma, whatever. This approach
has never let me down, and it has made all the
difference in my life."
~Steve Jobs was an American entrepreneur
and co-founder of Apple Inc.

75
"Beliefs have the power to create and the
power to destroy.
Human beings have the awesome ability to
take any experience of their lives and create a
meaning that disempowers them or one that can
literally save their lives."
~Tony Robbins is an American author,
entrepreneur,
Philanthropist and life coach

76
"Nothing in the world is more common than
unsuccessful people with talent."
~Unknown

77
"The greatest pleasure in life is doing what
people say you cannot do."
~Walter Bagehot was a British journalist and
businessman

78
"Respect your efforts, respect yourself.
Self-respect leads to self-discipline.
When you have both firmly under your belt,
that's real power."
~Clinton Eastwood Jr. is an American actor
and filmmaker

79
"Impossible is just a big word thrown around
by small men who find it easier to live in the
world they've been given than to explore the
power they have to change it.
Impossible is not a fact. It's an opinion.
Impossible is not a declaration. It's a dare.
Impossible is potential. Impossible is
temporary. Impossible is nothing."
~Muhammad Ali was an American
professional boxer and is widely regarded as one
of the most significant and celebrated sports
figures of the 20th century

80
"Today I will do what others won't, so
tomorrow I can accomplish what others can't."
~Jerry Rice is one of the best NFL players of
all time

81
"Talent is God-given. Be humble.
Fame is man-given. Be grateful.
Conceit is self-given. Be careful."
~John Wooden is the best UCLA head coach
of all time

82
"There may be people that have more talent
than you, but there's no excuse for anyone to
work harder than you do."
~Derek Jeter is the five World Series MLB
champion

83
"If you only ever give 90% in training then
you will only ever give 90% when it matters."
~Michael Owen is the international soccer
champion

84

"It's hard to beat a person who never gives
up.
Heroes get remembered, but legends never
die."
~Babe Ruth is arguably the best MLB player
of all time

85

"In 1995 I had $7 bucks in my pocket and
knew two things: I'm broke as hell and one day I
won't be.
You Can Achieve Anything!"
~Dwayne Johnson is an American actor,
producer, and professional wrestler

86

"You will never change your life until you
change something you do daily. The secret of
your success is found in your daily routine."
~John C Maxwell is an American author and
speaker

87

"Hard work beats talent when talent doesn't
work hard."
~Tim Notke is a High School Basketball
Coach

88

"Remembering that you are going to die is
the best way I know to avoid the trap of thinking
you have something to lose."
~Steve Jobs was an American entrepreneur
and co-founder of Apple Inc.

89

"The best way out is always through."
~Robert Frost was one of the best known of
all American poets

90

"The two most powerful warriors are patience
and time.
...so remember: great achievements take
time, there is no overnight success."
~Leo Tolstoy regarded as one of the greatest
authors of all time

91
"When you want to succeed as bad as you
want to breathe, then you'll be successful."
~Eric Thomas is an American motivational
speaker, author, and minister

92
"Work so hard that one day your signature
will be called an autograph."
~Tim Notke

93
"Pain is your friend; it is your ally. The best
thing about pain is: It tells you-you're not dead
yet!"
~G.I Jane American action film

94
"The power of imagination makes us
infinite."
~John Muir was a Scottish-American author

95

"Believe and act as if it were impossible to
fail."
~Charles Kettering was an American inventor
and the holder of 186 patents

96

"Without passion, you don't have energy.
Without energy, you have nothing."
~Warren Buffett is an American business
magnate and the fourth wealthiest person in the
world

97

"Some people want it to happen, some wish it
would happen, others make it happen."
~ Michael Jordan is considered as greatest
basketball player of all time

98

"The only thing standing between you and
your goal is the bullshit story you keep telling
yourself as to why you can't achieve it."
~Jordan Belfort is the author of
"Wolf of Wall Street"

99
"Nothing is worth more than this day."
~Johann Wolfgang was the author of
Conversations with Goethe

100
"The strongest oak of the forest is not the one
that is protected from the storm and hidden
from the sun.
It's the one that stands in the open where it is
compelled to struggle for its existence against
the wind and rains and the scorching sun."
~Napoleon Hill was an American self-help
author and famous for
"Think and Grow Rich"

101
"Always bear in mind that your own
resolution to succeed is more important than
any other one thing."
~Abraham Lincoln, 16th President of the
United States

102
"All that we are is the result of what we have thought.
If a man speaks or acts with an evil thought, pain follows him.
If a man speaks or acts with a pure thought, happiness follows him, like a shadow that never leaves him."
~Buddha was spiritual teacher from ancient India who founded Buddhism

103
"I am strong because I am weak.
I am beautiful because I know my flaws.
I am a lover because I am a fighter.
I am fearless because I have been afraid.
I am wise because I have been foolish.
& I can laugh because I've known sadness."
~Unknown

104
"That which does not kill us makes us stronger."
~Friedrich Nietzsche was a German philosopher

105
"Every time I thought I was being rejected
from something good, I was actually being re-
directed to something better."
~Steve Maraboli is a life-changing Speaker,
Bestselling Author, and Behavioral Scientist

106
"Courage is the discovery that you may not
win, and trying when you know you can lose"
~Tom Krause was a Finnish operatic bass-
baritone, particularly associated with Mozart
roles

107
"A river cuts through rock, not because of its
power, but because of its persistence."
~James Watkins is the author of Death &
Beyond and The Why Files series

108
"You learn nothing from life if you think
you're right all the time."
~Unknown

109

"No one can make you feel inferior without
your consent."
~Eleanor Roosevelt was the longest-serving
First Lady of the United States

110

"Don't look back, you're not going that way!"
~Marcia Karen Wallace was an American
actress and voice artist

111

"Nothing worth having comes easy."
~Theodore Roosevelt Jr. was served as the
26th President of the United States

112

"When you feel like quitting: think about why
you started."
~Unknown

113

"What we fear doing most is usually what we
most need to do."
~Timothy Ferriss, New York Times best-
selling author of 4-Hour Workweek

114
"Don't count the days, make the days count."
~Muhammad Ali was an American
professional boxer and is widely regarded as one
of the most significant and celebrated sports
figures of the 20th century

115
"Our greatest glory is not in never falling, but
in rising every time we fall."
~Confucius was a Chinese teacher, politician,
and philosopher

116
"I never lose. I either win or learn."
~Nelson Mandela was a South African anti-
apartheid revolutionary and served as President
of South Africa from 1994 to 1999

117
"Ever tried. Ever failed.
No matter. Try again.
Fail again. Fail better."
~Samuel Beckett was an Irish avant-garde
novelist and poet

118

"Seek patience and passion in equal amounts.
Patience alone will not build the temple.
Passion alone will destroy its walls."
~Maya Angelou was an American poet,
memoirist, and civil right activist

119

"The most beautiful people we have known
are those who have known defeat, known
suffering, known struggle, known loss, and have
found their way out of the depths.
These persons have an appreciation, a
sensitivity and an understanding of life that fills
them with compassion, gentleness, and a deep
loving concern. Beautiful people do not just
happen."
~Elisabeth Kübler-Ross was a Swiss-
American psychiatrist and the author of the
groundbreaking book
"On Death and Dying"

120

"What lies behind us and what lies before us
are tiny matters compared to what lies within
us."
~Ralph Waldo Emerson was an American
essayist, lecturer, and poet

121
"Sometimes it takes an overwhelming
breakdown to have an unbelievable Life ahead."
~Unknown

122
"The best day of your life is the one on which
you decide your life is your own.
No apologies or excuses.
No one to lean on, rely on, or blame.
The gift is yours it is an amazing journey and
you alone are responsible for the quality of it.
This is the day your life really begins."
~Bob Moawad is an author and motivational
speaker

123
"Follow your instincts.
That's where true wisdom manifests itself."
~Oprah Winfrey is an American media
proprietor, talk show host, actress and producer

124
"There are only two rules for being
successful.
One, figure out exactly what you want to do,
and two, do it."
~Mario Cuomo was an American Democratic
politician and served as the 52nd Governor of
New York for three terms

125
"Defeat is a state of mind; No one is ever
defeated until defeat has been accepted as a
reality."
~Bruce Lee was a Hong Kong and American
actor and founder of the martial art

126
"Acknowledging the good that you already
have in your life is the foundation for all
abundance."
~Eckhart Tolle is the author of
"The Power of Now and A New Earth:
Awakening to your Life's Purpose"

127
"Live life as though nobody is watching, and
express yourself as though everyone is
listening."
~Nelson Mandela was a South African anti-
apartheid revolutionary and served as President
of South Africa from 1994 to 1999

128
"Be yourself, but always your better self."
~Karl Maeser was a prominent Utah
educator and a member of The Church of Jesus
Christ of Latter-day Saints

129
"You don't have to be great to start, but you
do have to start to be great."
~Zig Ziglar was an American author and
motivational speaker

130
"Dream big, start small, but most of all,
start."
~Simon Sinek is a British/American author
and motivational speaker

131
"Take the first step in faith.
You don't have to see the whole staircase, just
take the first step."
~Martin Luther King Jr. was an American
Baptist minister and activist who became the
most visible spokesperson and leader in the
Civil Rights Movement

132
"The only impossible journey is the one you
never begin."
~Tony Robbins is an American author,
entrepreneur,
Philanthropist and life coach

133
"Successful people identify their life's core
purpose and relentlessly follow that purpose to
become the best representation of themselves
that they can become."
~Oprah Winfrey is an American media
proprietor, talk show host, actress and producer

134
"The difference between ordinary and
extraordinary is that little extra."
~Jimmy Johnson is an American football
broadcaster and former player

135
"Work on yourself more than you do on your
job."
~Jim Rohn was an American entrepreneur,
author, and motivational speaker

136
"When we strive to become better than we
are, everything around us becomes better too."
~Paulo Coelho is the author of The Alchemist

137
"Nurture your mind with great thoughts, for
you will never go any higher than you think."
~Benjamin Disraeli, 1st Earl of Beaconsfield
who twice served as Prime Minister of the
United Kingdom

138
"You must not only aim right but draw the
bow with all your might."
~Henry Thoreau was an American essayist,
philosopher and the author of Walden, a
reflection upon simple living in natural
surroundings

139
"Great spirits have always encountered
violent opposition from mediocre minds.
The mediocre mind is incapable of
understanding the man who refuses to bow
blindly to conventional prejudices and chooses
instead to express his opinions courageously
and honestly."
~Albert Einstein was a German-born
theoretical physicist and considered as one of
the most renowned scientists of all time

140
"There is only one way to avoid criticism: do
nothing, say nothing, and be nothing."
~Aristotle was an ancient Greek philosopher,
scientist and considered one of the greatest
intellectual figures of Western history

141
“God grant me the serenity to accept the
things I cannot change, the courage to change
the things I can, and the wisdom to know the
difference.”
~Reinhold Niebuhr was an American
theologian and worked as professor at Union
Theological Seminary

142
“If you’re always trying to be normal, you will
never know how amazing you can be.”
~Maya Angelou was an American poet,
memoirist, and civil right activist

143
“The only thing that is ultimately real about
your journey is the step that you are taking at
this moment. That’s all there ever is.”
~Eckhart Tolle is the author of The Power of
Now and A New Earth: Awakening to your Life’s
Purpose

144
"Do every act of your life as though it were
the last act of your life."
~Marcus Aurelius was Roman emperor from
161 to 180

145
"Everything is created twice, first in the mind
and then in reality."
~Robin Sharma is a Canadian writer and best
known for the book "The Monk Who Sold His
Ferrari"

146
"There is no greater agony than bearing an
untold story inside you."
~Maya Angelou was an American poet,
memoirist, and civil right activist

147
"Successful people have fear, successful
people have doubts, and successful people have
worries.
They just don't let these feelings stop them."
~T. Harv Eker is an author, businessman and
motivational speaker

148
"All the adversity I've had in my life, all my troubles and obstacles, have strengthened me... You may not realize it when it happens, but a kick in the teeth may be the best thing in the world for you."
~Walt Disney was an entrepreneur, animator, voice actor and co-founded The Walt Disney Company

149
"Inaction breeds doubt and fear.
Action breeds confidence and courage.
If you want to conquer fear, do not sit home and think about it.
Go out and get busy."
~Dale Carnegie was an American writer and very famous for the bestselling book "how to win friends and influence people"

150
"If your ship hasn't come in ... swim out to it."
~Mary Engelbreit is the founder of Home Companion magazine

151
"Be thankful for what you have; you'll end up
having more.
If you concentrate on what you don't have,
you will never, ever have enough."
~Oprah Winfrey is an American media
proprietor, talk show host, actress and producer

152
"I'm selfish, impatient and a little insecure.
I make mistakes, I am out of control and at
times hard to handle.
But if you can't handle me at my worst, then
you sure as hell don't deserve me at my best."
~Marilyn Monroe was an American actress
and became very famous for playing comic
"dumb blonde"

153
"In three words I can sum up everything I've
learned about life: it goes on."
~Robert Frost was one of the best known of
all American poets

154
"People don't buy what you do, they buy why
you do it."
~ Simon Sinek is a British/American author
and motivational speaker

155
"I believe that everything happens for a
reason.
People change so that you can learn to let go,
things go wrong so that you appreciate them
when they're right, you believe lies so you
eventually learn to trust no one but yourself,
and sometimes good things fall apart so better
things can fall together."
~Marilyn Monroe was an American actress
and became very famous for playing comic
"dumb blonde"

156
"I'm the happiest because I'm doing exactly
what I want to do"
~Gary Vaynerchuk is an American
entrepreneur, four-time New York Times
bestselling author

157

"If you can't fly, then run, if you can't run,
then walk, if you can't walk, then crawl, but by
all means keep moving forward."
~Martin Luther King Jr. was an American
Baptist minister and activist who became the
most visible spokesperson and leader in the
Civil Rights Movement

158

"Everything you've ever wanted is on the
other side of fear."
~George Adair is the Founder of
"Omega Vector"

159

"You gain strength, courage, and confidence
by every experience in which you really stop to
look fear in the face.
You are able to say to yourself, 'I have lived
through this horror.
I can take the next thing that comes along.'
You must do the thing you think you cannot
do."
~Eleanor Roosevelt was the longest-serving
First Lady of the United States

160
"I learned that courage was not the absence
of fear, but the triumph over it. The brave man
is not he who does not feel afraid, but he who
conquers that fear."
~Nelson Mandela was a South African anti-
apartheid revolutionary and served as President
of South Africa from 1994 to 1999

161
"There no longer has to be a difference
between who you are and what you do."
~Gary Vaynerchuk is an American
entrepreneur, four-time New York Times
bestselling author

162
"Give me six hours to chop down a tree and I
will spend the first four sharpening the axe."
~Abraham Lincoln, 16th President of the
United States

163
"We are what we repeatedly do.
Excellence, then, is not an act but a habit."
~Aristotle was an ancient Greek philosopher,
scientist and considered one of the greatest
intellectual figures of Western history

164
"You cannot change your destination
overnight,
But you can change your direction
overnight."
~Jim Rohn was an American entrepreneur,
author, and motivational speaker

165
"I think goals should never be easy, they
should force you to work, even if they are
uncomfortable at the time."
~Michael Phelps is an American retired
competitive swimmer and the most successful
Olympian of all time

166
"Fairy tales are more than true: not because
they tell us that dragons exist, but because they
tell us that dragons can be beaten."
~Neil Gaiman is an English author of novels
and best known for
"Stardust"

167
"Losers quit when they're tired.
Winners quit when they've won."
~Attributed to Mike Ditka, is a former
American football player

168
"You only have to do a very few things right
in your life so long as you don't do too many
things wrong."
~Warren Buffett is an American business
magnate and the fourth wealthiest person in the
world

169
"Most people give up just when they're about
to achieve success.
They quit on the one-yard line.
They give up at the last minute of the game,
one foot from a winning touchdown."
~H. Ross Perot was the founder of Electronic
Data Systems

170

"Knowing others is intelligence; knowing
yourself is true wisdom.
Mastering others is strength; mastering
yourself is true power."
~Lao Tzu was an ancient Chinese
philosopher and writer

171

"Passion is what gets you through the hardest
times that might otherwise make strong men
weak, or make you give up."
~Neil deGrasse Tyson is an American
astrophysicist, author, and science
communicator

172

"If you're not prepared to be wrong, you'll
never come up with anything original."
~Kenneth Robinson is a British author and
has been knighted for services to art

173
"I really don't think life is about the I-could-
have-been.
Life is only about the I-tried-to-do.
I don't mind the failure, but
I can't imagine that I'd forgive myself if I
didn't try."
~Nikki Giovanni is one of the world's most
well-known African-American poets

174
"Find out who you are and be that person.
That's what your soul was put on this Earth
to be. Find that truth, live that truth and
everything else will come."
~Ellen DeGeneres is an American comedian
and host of The Ellen DeGeneres Show

175
"You've got to follow your passion.
You've got to figure out what it is you love,
Who you really are. And have the courage to
do that.
I believe that the only courage anybody ever
needs
Is the courage to follow your own dreams."
~Oprah Winfrey is an American media
proprietor, talk show host, actress and producer

176
"I have not failed.
I've just found 10,000 ways that won't work."
~Thomas Edison was considered as
America's greatest inventor who invented the
electric light bulb

177
"We tend to forget that happiness doesn't
come
As a result of getting something we don't
have,
But rather of recognizing and appreciating
what we do have."
~Friedrich Koenig was a German inventor
best known for his high-speed steam-powered
printing press

178
"Death is not the greatest loss in life.
The greatest loss is what dies inside us while
we live."
~Norman Cousins was an American political
journalist and author

179
"Success is doing what you want, when you
want,
Where you want, with whom you want, as
much as you want."
~Tony Robbins is an American author,
entrepreneur,
Philanthropist and life coach

180
"Most of the important things in the world
Have been accomplished by people
Who have kept on trying,
When there seemed to be no hope at all."
~Dale Carnegie was an American writer and
very famous for the bestselling book "how to
win friends and influence people"

181
"For most of us the problem isn't that we aim
too high and fail - it's just the opposite - we aim
too low and succeed."
~Kenneth Robinson is a British author and
has been knighted for services to art

182
"I wouldn't say anything is impossible.
I think that everything is possible as long as
you put your mind to it and put the work and
time into it."
~Michael Phelps is an American retired
competitive swimmer and the most successful
Olympian of all time

183
"Somebody should tell us,
Right at the start of our lives,
That we are dying.
Then we might live life to the limit,
Every minute of every day.
Do it! I say.
Whatever you want to do, do it now!
There are only so many tomorrows."
~Pope Paul VI

184

"For a long time, it seemed to me that real life
was about to begin - real life.
But there was always some obstacle in the
way.
Something had to be got through first,
Some unfinished business,
Time still to be served, or a debt to be paid.
Then life would begin.
At last, it dawned on me that these obstacles
were my life."
~Albert D'Souza is the tenth Archbishop of
Agra India

185

"It's not whether you get knocked down.
It's whether you get up again."
~Vince Lombardi was an American football
player, coach, and executive in the national
football league

186

"A happy person is not a person in a certain
set of circumstances,
But rather a person with a certain set of
attitudes."
~Hugh Downs is a retired American
broadcaster and best known for hosting the
concentration game show

187
"Many of life's failures are people who did
not realize how close they were to success
When they gave up."
~Thomas Edison was considered as
America's greatest inventor who invented the
electric light bulb

188
"The best way to succeed is to double your
failure rate."
~Thomas John Watson Sr. was chairman of
IBM and known as one of the richest men of his
time

189
"Your time is limited, so don't waste it living
someone else's life.
Don't be trapped by dogma,
Which is living with the results of other
people's thinking.
Don't let the noise of other's opinions drown
out your own inner voice.
And most important, have the courage to
follow your heart and intuition. They somehow
Already know what you truly want to become.
Everything else is secondary.
~Steve Jobs was an American entrepreneur
and co-founder of Apple Inc.

190
"Courage doesn't mean you don't get afraid.
Courage means you don't let fear stop you."
~Bethany Hamilton is an American
professional surfer and wrote the autobiography
"Soul Surfer"

191
"No matter how many mistakes you make or
how slow you progress, you are still way ahead
of everyone who isn't trying."
~Tony Robbins is an American author,
entrepreneur,
Philanthropist and life coach

192
"You can only become truly accomplished at
something you love.
Don't make money your goal.
Instead, pursue the things you love doing,
And then do them so well that people can't
take their eyes off you."
~Maya Angelou was an American poet,
memoirist, and civil right activist

193
"Work like you don't need the money,
Love like your heart has never been broken,
And dance like no one is watching."
~Aurora Greenway, fictional character from
the movie Terms of Endearment

194
"If you light a lamp for someone else
It will also brighten your path."
~Buddha was spiritual teacher from ancient
India who founded Buddhism

195
"Don't be afraid to give your best to what
seemingly are small jobs.
Every time you conquer one it makes you that
much stronger.
If you do the little jobs well, the big ones will
tend to take care of themselves."
~Dale Carnegie was an American writer and
very famous for the bestselling book "how to
win friends and influence people"

196
"Darkness cannot drive out darkness; only
light can do that.
Hate cannot drive out hate; only love can do
that."
~Martin Luther King Jr. was an American
Baptist minister and activist who became the
most visible spokesperson and leader in the civil
rights movement

197
"So many people along the way, whatever it is
you aspire to do, will tell you it can't be done.
But all it takes is imagination.
You dream. You plan. You reach.
There will be obstacles.
There will be doubters.
There will be mistakes.
But with hard work, with belief, with
confidence and trust in yourself and those
around you, there are no limits."
~Michael Phelps is an American retired
competitive swimmer and the most successful
Olympian of all time

198
"The only way to do great work is to love
what you do.
If you haven't found it yet, keep looking.
Don't settle.
As with all matters of the heart, you'll know
when you find it."
~Steve Jobs was an American entrepreneur
and co-founder of Apple Inc.

199
"Love the life you live.
Live the life you love."
~Bob Marley was international musical and
cultural icon

200
"One day you will wake up and there won't be
any more time to do the things you've always
wanted.
Do it now."
~Paulo Coelho is the author of
"The Alchemist"

201

"I fear not the man who has practiced 10,000
kicks once, but I fear the man who has practiced
one kick 10,000 times."
~Bruce Lee was a Hong Kong and American
actor and founder of the martial art

202

"Eighty percent of success is showing up."
~Woody Allen is an American filmmaker and
considered as one of the greatest comedians

203

"Until a person can say deeply and honestly,
I am what I am today because of the choices
I made yesterday, that person cannot say, I
choose otherwise".
~Stephen Covey was an American author and
was most popular for The 7 Habits of Highly
Effective People

204
"Employ your time in improving yourself by other men's writings, so that you shall gain easily what others have labored hard for."
~Socrates was a classical Greek philosopher credited as one of the founders of Western philosophy

205
"Twenty years from now you will be more disappointed by the things that you didn't do than by the ones you did do.
So throw off the bowlines.
Sail away from the safe harbor.
Catch the trade winds in your sails.
Explore. Dream. Discover.
~Harriett Brown Jr. is an American author best known for his inspirational book "Life's Little Instruction Book"

206
"Give whatever you are doing and whoever you are with the gift of your attention."
~Jim Rohn was an American entrepreneur, author, and motivational speaker

207
"At any given moment you have the power to
say this is not how the story is going to end."
~Christine Miller is an author and artist

208
"The world has the habit of making room for
the man whose words and actions show that he
knows where he is going."
~Napoleon Hill was an American self-help
author and famous for
"Think and Grow Rich"

209
"People often say that motivation doesn't
last.
Well, neither does bathing, that's why we
recommend it daily."
~Zig Ziglar was an American author and
motivational speaker

210
"All our dreams can come true if we have the
courage to pursue them."
~Walt Disney was an entrepreneur,
animator, voice actor and co-founded The Walt
Disney Company

211

"And in the end, it's not the years in your life
that count.
It's the life in your years."
~Abraham Lincoln, 16th President of the
United States

212

"If you have built castles in the air, your work
need not be lost.
That is where they should be.
Now put the foundation under them."
~Henry Thoreau was an American essayist,
philosopher and the author of Walden, a
reflection upon simple living in natural
surroundings

213

"We don't see things as they are, we see them
as we are."
~Anais Nin was an American diarist, essayist,
novelist, and writer of short stories

214

"Man cannot discover new oceans unless he
has the courage to lose sight of the shore."
~Andre Gide was a French author and got
Nobel Prize for Literature in 1947

215
"We change our behavior when the pain of
staying the same becomes greater than the pain
of changing.
Consequences give us the pain that motivates
us to change.
~Henry Cloud is an American self-help
author who wrote "Boundaries: When to Say
Yes, How to Say No to Take Control of Your
Life"

216
"I've learned that people will forget what you
said, people will forget what you did, but people
will never forget how you made them feel."
~Maya Angelou was an American poet,
memoirist, and civil right activist

217
"A good plan violently executed now is better
than a perfect plan executed next week."
~Stephen Covey was an American author and
was most popular for
"The 7 Habits of Highly Effective People"

218
"Start where you are.
Use what you have.
Do what you can."
~Arthur Ashe was an American professional
tennis player who won three Grand Slam titles

219
"My interest in life comes from setting myself
huge, apparently unachievable challenges and
trying to rise above them."
~Sir Richard Branson is the founder of Virgin
Group, which controls more than 400
companies

220
"If you're going through hell, keep going!"
~Winston Churchill served as Prime Minister
of the United Kingdom from 1940 to 1945 and
again from 1951 to 1955

221
"You are not defined by your past.
You are prepared by your past."
~Joel Osteen is a televangelist in Texas and
the author of seven New York Times Best Sellers

222
"What you do has a far greater impact than
what you say."
~Stephen Covey was an American author and
was most popular for
"The 7 Habits of Highly Effective People"

223
"All great achievements require time."
~Maya Angelou was an American poet,
memoirist, and civil right activist

224
"Believe you can and you're halfway there."
~Theodore Roosevelt Jr. was served as the
26th President of the United States

225
"Discipline is the bridge between goals and
accomplishment."
~Jim Rohn was an American entrepreneur,
author, and motivational speaker

226
"Success is not final, failure is not fatal: it is
the courage to continue that counts."
~Winston Churchill served as Prime Minister
of the United Kingdom from 1940 to 1945 and
again from 1951 to 1955

227
"If you aim at nothing, you will hit it every
time."
~Zig Ziglar was an American author and
motivational speaker

228
"If you do what you've always done, you'll get
what you've always gotten."
~Tony Robbins is an American author,
entrepreneur,
Philanthropist and life coach

229
"I am not a product of my circumstances.
I am a product of my decisions."
~Stephen Covey was an American author and
was most popular for
"The 7 Habits of Highly Effective People"

230
"Happiness is not something ReadyMade. It
comes from your own actions."
~Tenzin Gyatso is the XIV Dalai Lama

231
"I attribute my success to this: I never gave or
took any excuse."
~Florence Nightingale was an English social
reformer and the founder of modern nursing

232
"It is absurd that a man should rule others,
who cannot rule himself."
~Latin Proverb

233
"Management is efficiency in climbing the
ladder of success; leadership determines
whether the ladder is leaning against the right
wall."
~Stephen Covey was an American author and
was most popular for
"The 7 Habits of Highly Effective People"

234
"The most important question to ask is, what
am I becoming?"
~Jim Rohn was an American entrepreneur,
author, and motivational speaker

235
"Every no gets me closer to a yes."
~Mark Cuban is a businessman and the
owner of the NBA's Dallas Mavericks

236
"What is not started today is never finished
tomorrow."
~Johann Wolfgang was the author of
Conversations with Goethe

237
"The difference between a successful person
and others is not a lack of strength, not a lack of
knowledge, but rather a lack in will."
~Vince Lombardi was an American football
player, coach, and executive in the National
Football League

238
"It is never too late to be what you might
have been."
~George Eliot was one of the leading writers
of the Victorian era

239
"The key is in not spending time, but in
investing it."
~Stephen Covey was an American author and
was most popular for
"The 7 Habits of Highly Effective People"

240
"Work like there is someone working 24
hours a day to take it away from you."
~Mark Cuban is a businessman and the
owner of the NBA's Dallas Mavericks

241
"Only those who will risk going too far can
possibly find out how far one can go."
~T.S. Eliot was one of the twentieth century's
major poets

242
"To live is the rarest thing in the world. Most people exist, that is all."
~Oscar Wilde was an Irish poet and best known for the novel
"The Picture of Dorian Gray"

243
"The road to success is always under construction."
~Lily Tomlin is an American actress, comedian, and writer

244
"Nobody can go back and start a new beginning, but anyone can start today and make a new ending."
~Maria Robinson was an Irish-British painter

245
"Remember That The Happiest People Are Not Those Getting More, But Those Giving More."
~Harriett Brown Jr. is an American author best known for his inspirational book
"Life's Little Instruction Book"

246

“There are no secrets to success.
It is the result of preparation, hard work, and
learning from failure.”
~Colin Powell is an American elder
statesman and a retired four-star general in the
United States Army

247

“I can’t change the direction of the wind, but
I can adjust my sails to always reach my
destination.”
~Jimmy Dean was an American country
music singer and best known today as the
creator of the Jimmy Dean sausage brand

248

“Action may not always bring happiness, but
there is no happiness without action.”
~Benjamin Disraeli, 1st Earl of Beaconsfield
who twice served as Prime Minister of the
United Kingdom

249
"Some people dream of success, while other people get up every morning and make it happen."
~Wayne Huizenga is an American businessman and entrepreneur

250
"You have to always be ready, always be alive, and always be willing to move in a new direction."
~Kevin Spacey is an American actor and got academy award for best actor for the "American Beauty"

251
"Happiness is not the absence of problems, it's the ability to deal with them."
~Steve Maraboli is a life-changing speaker, bestselling author, and behavioral scientist

252
"Strive not to be a success, but rather to be of value."
~Albert Einstein was a German-born theoretical physicist and considered as one of the most renowned scientists of all time

253
"If you want happiness for an hour take a
nap.
If you want happiness for a day – go fishing.
If you want happiness for a year – inherit a
fortune.
If you want happiness for a lifetime – help
someone else."
~Chinese Proverb

254
"I know the price of success: dedication, hard
work and an unremitting devotion to the things
you want to see happen."
~Frank Lloyd Wright was recognized by the
American Institute of Architects as
"The greatest American architect of all time"

255
"Everyone wants to live on top of the
mountain, but all the happiness and growth
occurs while you're climbing it."
~Andy Rooney was an American radio and
television writer and best known for his weekly
broadcast
"A Few Minutes with Andy Rooney"

256
"Your true success in life begins only when
you make the commitment to become excellent
at what you do."
~Brian Tracy is a Canadian-American
motivational public speaker and self-
development author

257
"Keep your eyes on the stars and your feet on
the ground."
~Theodore Roosevelt Jr. was served as the
26th President of the United States

258
"Happiness is when what you think, what you
say, and what you do are in harmony."
~Mahatma Gandhi was the leader of the
Indian independence movement against British
rule

259
"Success is not how high you have climbed,
but how you make a positive difference to the
world."
~Roy T. Bennett is the author of
"The Light in the Heart"

260
"People think I'm joking when I say that
whoever experiments the most in life wins. But
I'm not…"
~Tai Lopez is an investor, partner, and
advisor to over 20 multi-million dollar
businesses

261
"No matter how great the talent or efforts,
something just takes time.
You can't produce a baby in one month by
getting nine women pregnant."
~Warren Buffett is an American business
magnate and the fourth wealthiest person in the
world

262
"One of the secrets of a happy life is
continuous small treats."
~Iris Murdoch was an Anglo-Irish novelist
and the Times ranked her twelfth on a list of
"The 50 greatest British writers since 1945"

263
"Yesterday I was clever, so I wanted to
change the world.
Today I am wise, so I am changing myself."
~Rumi was a 13th-century Persian poet and
has been described as the "most popular poet"

264
"Obsessed is a word used often by the lazy, in
order to describe the dedicated."
~Tai Lopez is an investor, partner, and
advisor to over 20 multi-million dollar
businesses

265
"I cannot teach anybody anything.
I can only make them think"
~Socrates was a classical Greek philosopher
credited as one of the founders of Western
philosophy

266
"Remember this that very little is needed to
make a happy life."
~Marcus Aurelius was Roman emperor from
161 to 180

267
"Kites rise highest against the wind, not with
it."
~Winston Churchill served as Prime Minister
of the United Kingdom from 1940 to 1945 and
again from 1951 to 1955

268
"We fear the future because we are wasting
the today"
~Mother Teresa was a Roman Catholic nun
who devoted her life to serving the poor

269
"You never know how strong you are, until
being strong is your only choice."
~Bob Marley was international musical and
cultural icon

270
"Children are happy because they don't have
a file in their minds called
All the Things That Could Go Wrong."
~Marianne Williamson is an American
spiritual author and the founder of
"Project Angel Food"

271
"Remember that your brain isn't built for
happiness.
It's built for survival.
Happiness is something you have to create
after-the-fact."
~Tai Lopez is an investor, partner, and
advisor to over 20 multi-million dollar
businesses

272
"We learn from failure, not from success!"
~Bram Stoker was an Irish author who wrote
the book "Dracula"

273
"...God's love is so real that He created you to
prove it."
~Nick Vujicic is best-selling author,
motivational speaker, and evangelist

274
"Attitude is a choice. Happiness is a choice.
Optimism is a choice. Kindness is a choice.
Giving is a choice.
Respect is a choice.
Whatever choice you make makes you.
Choose wisely."
~Roy T. Bennett is the author of
"The Light in the Heart"

275
"In this life, to earn your place you have to
fight for it."
~Shakira is the highest-selling Colombian
artist of all time

276
"Working hard for something we don't care
about is called stress; working hard for
something we love is called passion."
~ Simon Sinek is a British/American author
and motivational speaker

277
"You will always grow through, what you go
through."
~Tyrese Gibson is an American singer and
actor

278
"The best way to cheer yourself is to try to
cheer someone else up."
~Samuel Langhorne Clemens better known
by his pen name Mark Twain, was an American
writer and humorist

279
"Great works are performed not by strength,
but perseverance."
~Dr. Samuel Johnson was an English writer
who is described by the Oxford Dictionary of
National Biography as "arguably the most
distinguished man of letters in English history"

280
"People become successful the minute they
decide to."
~Harvey Mackay is a businessman and
author of 7 New York Times bestselling books

281
"Winning is not a "sometimes" thing. You don't win once in a while, you don't do things right once in a while, you do them right all of the time.
Winning is a habit, unfortunately, so is losing."
~Vince Lombardi was an American football player, coach, and executive in the National Football League

282
"The grand essentials to happiness in this life are something to do, something to love, and something to hope for."
~George Washington Burnap was the author of
"The Sphere and Duties of Woman: A Course of Lectures"

283
"The fastest way to pass your own expectations is to add passion to your labor."
~Mike Litman is the author of
"Conversations with Millionaires"

284
"Accept the past for what it was.
Acknowledge the present for what it is.
Anticipate the future for what it can become.
~Tracy L. McNair is a writer who born in
Corley family

285
"If you have a burning desire and a plan to
take action, there is absolutely nothing you
cannot achieve."
~Thomas J. Vilord is a public speaker and
author

286
"Be grateful for what you already have while
you pursue your goals.
If you aren't grateful for what you already
have, what makes you think you would be happy
with more."
~Roy T. Bennett is the author of
"The Light in the Heart"

287
"If you think you can or if you think you can't,
either way, you are right."
~Tony Robbins is an American author,
entrepreneur,
Philanthropist and life coach

288
"People are anxious to improve their
circumstances but are unwilling to improve
themselves.
That is why they remain bound."
~James Allen was a British philosophical
writer and best known for the book
"As a Man Thinketh"

289
"If you want others to be happy, practice
compassion. If you want to be happy, practice
compassion."
~Tenzin Gyatso is the XIV Dalai Lama

290
"Take responsibility for your own happiness,
never put it in other people's hands."
~Roy T. Bennett is the author of "The Light
in the Heart"

291
"People become really quite remarkable when
they start thinking that they can do things.
When they believe in themselves, they have the
first secret of success."
~Norman Vincent Peale was an American
author and best known for his best-selling book
"The Power of Positive Thinking"

292
"If you set your goals ridiculously high and
it's a failure, you will fail above everyone else's
success"
~James Cameron is a Canadian filmmaker
and holds the distinction of having directed two
of the three films in history to gross over $2
billion worldwide.

293
"People think focus means saying yes to the
thing you've got to focus on.
But that's not what it means at all.
It means saying no to the hundred other good
ideas that there are.
You have to pick carefully.
I'm actually as proud of the things we haven't
done as the things I have done.
Innovation is saying no to 1,000 things."
~Steve Jobs was an American entrepreneur
and co-founder of Apple Inc.

294
"Happiness is the meaning and the purpose
of life, the whole aim, and end of human
existence."
~Aristotle was an ancient Greek philosopher,
scientist and considered one of the greatest
intellectual figures of Western history

295
"What you seek is seeking you."
~Rumi was a 13th-century Persian poet and
has been described as the "most popular poet"

296
"I can't give you a surefire formula for
success, but I can give you a formula for failure:
try to please everybody all the time."
~Herbert Bayard Swope was an American
editor and the "first recipient of the Pulitzer
Prize"

297
"Named must your fear be before banish it
you can."
~Yoda is a fictional character in the Star
Wars and considered the most powerful Jedi
Master in the movie

298
"The more you feed your mind with positive
thoughts, the more you can attract great things
into your life."
~Roy T. Bennett is the author of
"The Light in the Heart"

299
"Do not seek to follow in the footsteps of the
wise, instead, seek what they sought."
~Matsuo Bashō was the most famous poet of
the Edo period in Japan

300
"Talk less, listen more."
~Brené Brown is the author of four New York
Times bestsellers

301
"There's only one way to the top: hard work."
~Charlie Munger is vice chairman of
Berkshire Hathaway with a net worth of
US$1.56 billion on August 2017

302
"Never give up. Today is hard, tomorrow will
be worse, but the day after tomorrow will be
sunshine."
~ Jack Ma is the Chairman of Alibaba Group
and the richest man in China

303
"It is important to remember, there are no
overnight successes. You will need to be
dedicated, single-minded, and there is no
substitute for hard work."
~Mukesh Ambani is an Indian business
magnate and the richest man in India with a net
worth of US$38 billion in 2017

304
"The greatest tragedy in life is not death, but
a life without a purpose."
~Myles Munroe was a Bahamian evangelist
and International Bestselling Author

305
"All you are or ever shall become is the result
of the use to which you put your mind."
~Napoleon Hill was an American self-help
author and famous for
"Think and Grow Rich"

306
"Even if you cannot change all the people
around you, you can change the people you
choose to be around.
Life is too short to waste your time on people
who don't respect, appreciate, and value you.
Spend your life with people who make you
smile, laugh, and feel loved."
~Roy T. Bennett is the author of
"The Light in the Heart"

307
“Of the billionaires I have known, money just
brings out the basic traits in them.
If they were jerks before they had money,
they are simply jerks with a billion dollars.”
~Warren Buffett is an American business
magnate and the fourth wealthiest person in the
world

308
“Behind every successful person lies a pack of
haters.”
~Marshall Bruce Mathers III, known
professionally as Eminem, is an American
rapper and he is the best-selling artist of the
2000s in the United States

309
“I’ve worked all my life on the subject of
awareness, whether it’s awareness of the body,
awareness of the mind, awareness of your
emotions, awareness of your relationships, or
awareness of your environment.
I think the key to transforming your life is to
be aware of who you are.”
~Deepak Chopra, is an American author,
public speaker and wealthiest figures in
alternative medicine

310

"Happiness is not a goal...it's a by-product of
a life well lived."
~Eleanor Roosevelt was the longest-serving
First Lady of the United States

311

"If my mind can conceive it and my heart can
believe it, then I can achieve it."
~Muhammad Ali was an American
professional boxer and is widely regarded as one
of the most significant and celebrated sports
figures of the 20th century

312

"I didn't come here to be average."
~ Michael Jordan is considered as greatest
basketball player of all time

313

"Worrying gets you nowhere.
If you turn up worrying about how you're
going to perform, you've already lost. Train
hard, turn up, run your best and the rest will
take care of itself."
~Usain Bolt retired Jamaican sprinter and
the first person to hold both the 100 meters and
200 meters world records

314
"For me, life is continuously being hungry.
The meaning of life is not simply to exist, to
survive, but to move ahead, to go up, to achieve,
to conquer."
~Arnold Schwarzenegger is an actor,
politician, and former professional bodybuilder
and served two terms as the 38th Governor of
California

315
"You must lose everything in order to gain
anything."
~Brad Pitt is an American actor and producer

316
"Victory is sweetest when you've known
defeat."
~Malcolm Forbes was an American
entrepreneur most prominently known as the
publisher of Forbes magazine

317
"I hated every minute of training, but I said,
'Don't quit. Suffer now and live the rest of your
life as a champion.'"
~Muhammad Ali was an American
professional boxer and is widely regarded as one
of the most significant and celebrated sports
figures of the 20th century

318
"You may have to fight a battle more than
once to win it."
~Margaret Thatcher was a British
stateswoman who served as Prime Minister of
the United Kingdom from 1979 to 1990

319
"To accomplish great things, we must not
only act but also dream, not only plan but also
believe."
~Anatole France was a French poet,
journalist, and novelist

320
"A lion runs fastest when he is hungry"
~Salman Khan is an Indian film actor and
producer

321
"Success isn't always about "Greatness", it's
about consistency.
Consistent, hard work gains success.
Greatness will come."
~Dwayne Johnson is an American actor,
producer, and professional wrestler

322
"The secret to success: find something you
love to do so much, you can't wait for the sun to
rise to do it all over again."
~Chris Gardner is an American
Entrepreneur, motivational speaker and author
of
"The Pursuit of Happyness"

323
"Strength does not come from winning. Your
struggles develop your strengths. When you go
through hardships and decide not to surrender,
that is strength."
~Arnold Schwarzenegger is an actor,
politician, and former professional bodybuilder
and served two terms as the 38th Governor of
California

324
"It doesn't matter how many times you have
failed, you only have to be right once."
~Mark Cuban is a businessman and the
owner of the NBA's Dallas Mavericks

325
"All your dreams await just on the other side
of your fears."
~Grant Cardone is the bestselling author of
"The 10X Rule and If You're Not First, You're
Last"

326
"Only you and you alone can change your
situation. Don't blame it on anything or
anyone."
~Leonardo DiCaprio is an American actor,
film producer, and environmental activist

327
"The devil whispers to the warrior
You cannot withstand the storm
The warrior replies
I AM THE STORM"
~Unknown

328
"If you want to be a leader who attracts
quality people, the key is to become a person of
quality yourself."
~Jim Rohn was an American entrepreneur,
author, and motivational speaker

329
"To be yourself in a world that is constantly
trying to make you something else is the
greatest accomplishment."
~Ralph Waldo Emerson was an American
essayist, lecturer, and poet

330
"He who is not courageous enough to take
risks will accomplish nothing in life."
~Muhammad Ali was an American
professional boxer and is widely regarded as one
of the most significant and celebrated sports
figures of the 20th century

331
"Life isn't about finding yourself. Life is about
creating yourself."
~George Bernard Shaw was an Irish
playwright, critic and the only person who has
won both an Academy Award and a Nobel Prize

332
"Put your heart, mind, and soul into even
your smallest acts. This is the secret of success."
~Swami Sivananda was a Hindu spiritual
teacher and a proponent of Yoga and Vedanta

333
"You are the average of the five people you
spend the most time with."
~Jim Rohn was an American entrepreneur,
author, and motivational speaker

334
"The happiness of your life depends upon the
quality of your thoughts."
~Marcus Aurelius was Roman emperor from
161 to 180

335
"Champions aren't made in gyms.
Champions are made from something they
have deep inside them-a desire, a dream, a
vision.
They have to have the skill and the will.
But the will must be stronger than the skill."
~Muhammad Ali was an American
professional boxer and is widely regarded as one
of the most significant and celebrated sports
figures of the 20th century

336
“Great minds discuss ideas; average minds
discuss events; small minds discuss people.”
~Attributed to Eleanor Roosevelt, was the
longest-serving First Lady of the United States

337
“‘Someday’ is a disease that will take your
dreams to the grave with you.”
~Timothy Ferriss, New York Times best-
selling author of 4-Hour Workweek

338
“Whatever you hold in your mind on a
consistent basis is exactly what you will
experience in your life.”
~Tony Robbins is an American author,
entrepreneur,
Philanthropist and life coach

339
“The greatest sin is to think yourself weak”
~Swami Vivekananda was an Indian Hindu
monk and considered as a key figure in the
introduction of the Indian philosophies of
Vedanta and Yoga to the Western world

340
"If you are not willing to learn, no one can
help you.
If you are determined to learn, no one can
stop you."
~Zig Ziglar was an American author and
motivational speaker

341
"There ain't nothing I can't do.
No sky too high, no sea too rough.
Anything in life worth doing is worth
overdoing.
Moderation is for cowards."
~Lone Survivor American biographical war
film

342
"The only way to get what you want in this
world is through hard work."
~Tiana, The Princess, and the Frog American
animated musical film

343
"The way to get started is to quit talking and start doing."
~Walt Disney was an entrepreneur, animator, voice actor and co-founded The Walt Disney Company

344
"Every great story on the planet happened when someone decided not to give up, but kept going no matter what."
~Spryte Loriano is Entrepreneur, spiritual explorer, humanitarian

345
"You don't learn to walk by following rules. You learn by doing and falling over."
~Sir Richard Branson is the founder of Virgin Group, which controls more than 400 companies

346
"As long as you're going to be thinking anyway, think big."
~Donald Trump is the 45th and current President of the United States

347
"If you're only willing to do what's easy, life
will be hard.
But if you're willing to do what's hard, life
will be easy."
~T. Harv Eker is an author, businessman and
motivational speaker

348
"In the confrontation between the stream and
the rock, the stream always wins, not through
strength, but through persistence."
~Buddha was spiritual teacher from ancient
India who founded Buddhism

349
"It's not what you achieve, it's what you
overcome.
That's what defines your career."
~Carlton Fisk is a retired Major League
Baseball catcher and a member of the Baseball
Hall of Fame

350
"The price of success is hard work, dedication
to the job at hand, and the determination that
whether we win or lose, we have applied the
best of ourselves to the task at hand."
~Vince Lombardi was an American football
player, coach, and executive in the National
Football League

351
"I am building a house where the floor is
made up of strength, where the walls are crafted
of ambition, where the roof is a masterpiece of
forgiveness. I am building myself."
~Noor Unnahar is a modern-day artist, poet
and the author of the book
"Yesterday I Was The Moon"

352
"I don't like to lose at anything…
Yet I've grown most not from victories, but
setbacks.
If winning is God's reward, then losing is how
he teaches us."
~Serena Williams is an American
professional tennis player and has ranked
world's No. 1 in singles on eight separate
occasions over the last 15 years by Women's
Tennis Association (WTA)

353
"Never be ashamed of a scar.
It simply means you were stronger than
whatever tried to hurt you."
~Unknown

354
"Do not judge me by my successes, judge me
by how many times I fell down and got back up
again."
~Nelson Mandela was a South African anti-
apartheid revolutionary and served as President
of South Africa from 1994 to 1999

355
"You have power over your mind "not outside events".
Realize this, and you will find strength."
~Marcus Aurelius was Roman emperor from 161 to 180

356
"Everyone can perform magic, everyone can reach his goals if he is able to think, if he is able to wait, if he is able to fast."
~Hermann Hesse was a German-born novelist and best-known the book "Siddhartha"

357
You might have more talent than me, you might be smarter than me, you might be sexier than me; you might be all of those.
But if we get on the treadmill together, there are two things: You're getting off first, or I'm going to die. It's really that simple, right? ...
You're not going to outwork me."
~Will Smith is an American actor and according to Newsweek April 2007 he is "the most powerful actor in Hollywood"

358
"Walk on with hope in your heart, and you'll
never walk alone"
~Shah Rukh Khan is an Indian film actor,
producer and referred by media as "King of
Bollywood"

359
"In the future, you're only going to be paid
for performance.
You won't be paid for your time anymore."
~Eric Worre is a writer, producer and best
known for the Documentary "Rise of the
Entrepreneur: The Search for a Better Way"

360
"True happiness comes not when we get rid
of all of our problems, but when we change our
relationship to them when we see our problems
as a potential source of awakening,
opportunities to practice, and to learn."
~Richard Carlson was an American author
and very famous for his book,
"Don't Sweat the Small Stuff... and it's all
Small Stuff"

361

"Before you speak, listen.
Before you write, think.
Before you spend, earn.
Before you invest, investigate.
Before you criticize, wait.
Before you pray, forgive.
Before you quit, try.
Before you retire, save.
Before you die, give."
~William A. Ward is one of America's most
quoted writers of inspirational maxims

362

"By three methods we may learn wisdom:
first, by reflection, which is noblest; second, by
imitation, which is easiest; and third by
experience, which is the bitterest."
~Confucius was a Chinese teacher, politician,
and philosopher

363

"If you seek peace, be still.
If you seek wisdom, be silent.
If you seek love, be yourself."
~Becca Lee is the author of
"A Perfect Moment"

364
"Life doesn't reward the naturally clever or
strong but those who can learn to fight and
work hard and never quit.
~Edward Michael "Bear" Grylls is a
Northern Irish adventurer and is widely known
for his television series
"Man vs. Wild"

365
"The greater the struggle the more glorious
the triumph"
~Nick Vujicic is best-selling author,
motivational speaker, and evangelist

366
"And once the storm is over, you won't
remember how you made it through, how you
managed to survive.
You won't even be sure, whether the storm is
really over.
But one thing is certain.
When you come out of the storm, you won't
be the same person who walked in.
That's what this storm's all about."
~Haruki Murakami is a Japanese writer and
very famous for the book
"A Wild Sheep Chase"

All you want to achieve is possible,
now all you need is to work hard and
Leave no stone unturned.
I wish you the best of luck on your
journey with most inspiring lines from
Chief Tecumseh

So live your life that the fear of death
can never enter your heart.
Trouble no one about their religion;
respect others in their view, and demand
that they respect yours.
Love your life, perfect your life, and
beautify all things in your life.
Seek to make your life long and its
purpose in the service of your people.
Prepare a noble death song for the day
when you go over the great divide.
Always give a word or a sign of salute
when meeting or passing a friend, even a
stranger, when in a lonely place.
Show respect to all people and grovel
to none.

When you arise in the morning give
thanks for the food and for the joy of

living.
If you see no reason for giving thanks,
the fault lies only in yourself.
Abuse no one and no thing, for abuse
turns the wise ones to fools and robs the
spirit of its vision.

When it comes your time to die, be not
like those whose hearts are filled with the
fear of death, so that when their time
comes they weep and pray for a little
more time to live their lives over again in
a different way.
Sing your death song and die like a
hero going home.

About the author

Sneha Rawat is an Arts Graduate(Gold Medalist) and has a Master's Degree in Management.
She is a voracious reader and writer.
She is currently working in the publishing industry.
She is the founder of Rudravan pub Pvt. limited and Bhoomi Infratech Pvt. limited.
Her rich and creative imagination made her follow writing and providing moral education for the young minds.

ACKNOWLEDGMENTS

I am fortunate to have many friends and every one of them has been approached by me for information or suggestions. A few individuals played a major role in making the book happen. My thanks go first to Divya Saxena, who urged me into this project. Akshara Dhaundiyal has rallied round to help me through hectic months, providing wisdom and sharp critical eye. I had not imagined that an editor could do as much as Akshara did. Illustrations are "Designed by Freepik".